Breakfast of Champions

Favorite Recipes to Start the Day

- Sandra G. McNish -

Overnight summer oats with roasted nectarines

Prep: 10 Min   Cook: 15 Min   Serves: 4

- 2/3 cup natural sliced almonds
- 1 cup rolled oats
- 1 large Granny Smith apple, quartered, cored, grated
- 2 cups unsweetened almond milk
- ½ cup sultanas
- ¼ cup currants
- 3 nectarines, cut into 12 wedges
- ¼ cup maple syrup, plus extra to drizzle
- Extra unsweetened almond milk, to serve (optional)

Method:

1. Roughly chop 1/3 cup almonds and place into a bowl. Add rolled oats, apple, almond milk, sultanas and currants. Stir until combined. Cover and refrigerate overnight.
2. Preheat oven to 200°C/180°C fan forced. Line a baking tray with baking paper. Combine nectarine wedges and maple syrup in a bowl. Spread on prepared baking tray and bake for 15 minutes or until nectarines are golden and softened. Spread remaining almonds on a second tray and bake for the last 5 minutes of cooking
3. Stir extra milk into porridge, if you like, and spoon into serving bowls. Top with roasted nectarines and almonds. Drizzle with extra maple syrup

Peanut butter, Cacao and Banana Smoothie

Prep: 5 Minutes   Serves: 1

*This almond milk smoothie is good enough to enjoy at any time of day. For those who are looking to indulge a little, look no further.

- 1 cup chilled Vitasoy Original Almond Milk
- 1 frozen peeled banana
- 1 tablespoon smooth peanut butter
- 1 tablespoon cacao powder
- Handful of ice

Method:

1. Place all ingredients into a blender.
2. Blend until smooth and serve.

Green eggs & ham

Prep: 5 Min   Cook: 10 Min   Serves: 4

Ingredients:

- 8 eggs
- 2 teaspoons olive oil
- 25g (1/3 cup) grated parmesan cheese
- 120g baby spinach
- 4 seeded brioche buns, split, toasted
- 80g thinly sliced lean leg ham

Method:

1. Place eggs, 100g spinach and parmesan into a blender and blend until combined. Season with salt and pepper.
2. Heat a large non-stick frying pan over medium heat until hot. Add the oil and swirl to coat pan base. Add egg mixture and cook for 1½ minutes or until mixture starts to set. Using a spatula, push set egg towards centre of pan, tilting pan to allow uncooked egg to run over base. Cook for 2 minutes or until eggs form creamy curds.
3. Top bun base with spinach leaves, ham and green eggs. Sprinkle with parmesan, top with bun lids to serve.

Egg Muffins three ways

Prep: 15 Mins   Cook: 25 Mins   Makes: 6

Ingredients:

- 6 eggs
- 1/2 cup milk
- 2 tbs plain flour
- 250g tomatoes, quartered, deseeded, diced
- 150g fetta, crumbled
- 2 tbs finely chopped chives
- 100g broccolini, roughly chopped
- 1 large carrot, grated
- 3/4 cup frozen peas
- 3/4 cup grated cheddar cheese
- 2 zucchini, grated
- 2 x 125g sweet corn kernels, drained
- 3/4 cup grated mozzarella

MUFFIN BASE

Preheat oven to 180°C. Line 6 Texas muffin moulds with paper cases. Whisk eggs, milk and flour in a medium bowl. Season with salt and white pepper. Add one of the fillings and spoon into prepared muffin cases. Bake for 20-25 minutes or until puffed and cooked through. Transfer to a wire rack to cool. Serve or wrap cold muffins in plastic wrap. Place wrapped muffins into clip lock bags or airtight containers and place in freezer for up to 2 months

TOMATO, FETA AND CHIVES

Add chopped tomatoes, fetta and chives to egg mixture. Season with salt and pepper

CHEESE AND VEG

Add broccolini, carrot and peas to a saucepan of boiling water. Cook for 2 minutes or until just tender. Drain and rinse under cold water. Drain well and add to egg mixture with cheese. Season with salt and pepper

ZUCCHINI, CORN AND MOZZARELLA

Grate zucchini and using your hands, squeeze as much liquid as possible from zucchini. Add zucchini, corn and mozzarella to egg mixture

The Best Pancakes

Prep: 10 Mins   Cook: 20 Mins   Makes: 12 Pancakes

Ingredients:

- 1 ½ cups plain flour
- 1 tablespoon baking powder
- 1 tablespoon caster sugar
- 3 eggs
- 1 cup milk
- 50g unsalted butter, melted
- 1 teaspoon vanilla extract (optional)
- Maple syrup, to serve
- Blueberries, to serve

Method:

1. In a large bowl, whisk the flour baking powder, sugar and a pinch of salt together. In a large jug whisk eggs, milk, butter and vanilla, if using. Make a well in the centre of the dry ingredients and whisk in milk mixture to make a smooth batter.

2. Heat a large, lightly greased non-stick frying pan over medium heat. Working in batches of 3, pour ¼ cups of batter into the pan. Cook pancakes for 1-2 minutes, until bubbles break on the surface and underside is golden brown. Flip over and cook for 1 minute.

3. Stack and serve the pancakes with maple syrup and blueberries.

Breakfast Focaccia

Prep: 10 Min, Plus 1 ½ Hours Proving Time Cook: 25 Minutes Serves: 8

Ingredients:
- 4 cups (600g) bread flour
- 2 tsp dry active yeast
- 1 tbsp sea salt
- 1 ¾ cups (430mls) warm water
- ½ cup (125ml) olive oil, plus extra for greasing
- 8 eggs 1 cup (100g) grated cheddar cheese
- 150g middle cut bacon, cut into thin strips
- ½ small red onion, cut into thin wedges
- 3-4 fresh rosemary sprigs

Method:

1. Place flour, yeast, 2 tsp salt in a large mixing bowl. Add warm water and 2 tbsp of the olive oil. Using clean hands, bring mixture together to form a wet and sticky dough. Add a little more oil to bowl and grease mixing bowl. Turn dough in bowl to coat. Cover and set aside in a warm place until it doubles in size (approx. 1 hour)
2. Pour remaining olive oil into a large 30cm x 40cm baking dish and swirl to coat evenly
3. Punch dough to expel air and place inside oiled baking dish. Using your fingertips, stretch the dough to the edges. Cover again and set aside in a warm place to puff up, (approx. 30 minutes)
4. Arrange oven rack in the middle position of the oven and preheat oven 240°C/220°C (fan-forced)
5. Using the base of a small glass dusted in flour, press down into dough to make 8 evenly spaced indents. Open out indents more by pushing the dough back with your fingers. Sprinkle with 2 tsp sea salt and scatter over cheese, bacon, onion and rosemary around the indents
6. Bake 15 minutes. Remove from oven and press the same glass into the indents to make them deeper. Crack 1 egg into each indent. Bake for a further 7- 9 minutes or until egg whites are set and yolks runny. Serve warm

Breakfast Egg and Salmon Bagels

Prep: 15 Minutes   Cook: 5-6 Minutes   Serves: 4

Ingredients:

- 6 eggs, at room temperature
- 1/3 cup milk
- 2 tbs finely chopped chives
- 4 fresh plain bagels, split
- 2 tbs butter, chopped
- 1/3 cup light spreadable cream cheese
  100g sliced smoked salmon
- Lemon wedges, to serve

Method:

1. Whisk eggs, milk and chives in a bowl until well combined. Set aside for a few minutes to allow foam to settle. Meanwhile, toast bagels
2. Heat a medium non-stick frying pan over medium heat. Add butter, melt and swirl to coat pan base. Add egg mixture and cook without stirring for 30 seconds
3. Using a wide spatula, push the set eggs around outer edge toward the centre of the pan, tilting the pan to allow the uncooked egg to run over the base
4. Gently push eggs around pan every 15 seconds until soft folds form and one quarter mixture is unset. Remove from heat. Gently fold the egg mixture once more
5. Spread toasted bagels with cream cheese. Top with smoked salmon and scrambled eggs. Season to taste. Serve with lemon wedges

Pancake Topping Ideas

Prep: 10 Mins   Cook: 20 Mins   Makes: 12

Ingredients:

PANCAKES

- 1 ½ cups plain flour
- 1 tablespoon baking powder
- 1 tablespoon caster sugar
- 3 eggs
- 1 cup milk
- 50g unsalted butter, melted
- 1 teaspoon vanilla extract (optional)

PANCAKE TOPPINGS

1. Coconut yoghurt, granola and nectarine
2. Mascarpone, raspberries and passionfruit curd
3. Cream cheese and strawberry compote
4. Ricotta, baby rocket, roast cherry tomatoes and balsamic glaze
5. Garlic mushrooms, Persian fetta and chives
6. Fried egg, kimchi and chilli sauce

Method:

PANCAKES

1. In a large bowl, whisk the flour baking powder, sugar and a pinch of salt together. In a large jug whisk eggs, milk, butter and vanilla, if using. Make a well in the centre of the dry ingredients and whisk in milk mixture to make a smooth batter
2. Heat a large, lightly greased non-stick frying pan over medium heat. Working in batches of 3, pour ¼ cups of batter into the pan. Cook pancakes for 1-2 minutes, until bubbles break on the surface and underside is golden brown. Flip over and cook for 1 minute
3. Stack and serve the pancakes with maple syrup and blueberries. Or choose from one of our sweet and savoury topping ideas

PANCAKE TOPPINGS

1. Add a dollop of yoghurt to your pancake. Top with a scattering of granola and slices of nectarine.
2. Spread pancakes with mascarpone and top with a tumble of raspberries and drizzle with passionfruit curd.
3. Add a smear of cream cheese to your pancake and top with a strawberry compote.
4. Spread pancake with ricotta. Top with spinach, cherry tomatoes and add a drizzle of balsamic.
5. Top your pancake with garlic mushrooms, a few cubes of fetta and a scatter of chopped chives.
6. Fry an egg and add it to your pancake. Top with good teaspoon of kimchi and drizzle with chilli sauce.

Egg and Smoked Trout Croissants

Prep: 10 Mins   Cook: 5 Mins   Serves: 4

Ingredients:

- 1 tablespoon extra virgin olive oil
- 4 eggs
- 4 large croissants
- ½ cup crème fraiche
- 1 tablespoon chopped chives, plus extra to serve
- ½ lemon, grated zest and
- 2 tsp of juice
- 1 cup watercress
- 100g smoked ocean trout slices
  Lemon wedges, to serve

Method:

1. Heat oil in a large non-stick frying pan on medium high. Crack eggs one at a time into hot pan. Cook for 2 minutes, until whites set and are crispy around the edges
2. Split croissants in half and place cut-side up on an oven tray lined with baking paper. Cook under grill for 30 seconds to 1 minute, until toasted and golden
3. In a small bowl, combine crème fraiche, chives, lemon zest and juice. Season with salt and pepper and mix well
4. Spread bases with crème fraiche mixture. Top with watercress, folds of trout slices and then a fried egg. Scatter with extra chives and pepper. Serve with lemon wedges and any extra crème fraiche mixture

Hash brown ham and egg nests

Prep: 20 Minutes Cook: 50 Minutes Serves: 6

Ingredients:

- 150g leftover Christmas ham, finely chopped, plus extra to serve
- 700g (about 2 large) potatoes, peeled and grated 1 tablespoon olive oil
- 20g (¼ cup) grated parmesan Salt and pepper
- 12 eggs
- 1 tablespoon finely chopped chives
- Finely grated parmesan, to serve

Method:

1. Preheat oven to 180°C fan forced. Grease a 12-hole non-stick (1/3 cup-capacity) muffin pan.
2. Heat a large, lightly greased non-stick frying pan over medium heat. Cook ham for 4 minutes or until golden and crisp. Drain on paper towel.
3. Place peeled and grated potato in a colander and squeeze out all moisture. Transfer to a large bowl and add oil, parmesan and half the ham. Season with salt and pepper.
4. Divide the potato mixture into each muffin hole, pressing into base and up the sides with the back of a spoon.
5. Bake for 20–25 minutes. Crack an egg into each hash brown cup one and bake for a further 8–10 minutes or egg whites are cooked and egg yolk is just setting.
6. Scatter hash brown egg cups with chives, parmesan and remaining ham.

Choc Pear Smoothie

Prep: 5 Minutes   Serves: 2

Make this healthy chocolate smoothie recipe with pears and cacao. This chocolate lovers smoothie is also sweetened with dates.

Ingredients:

- 1-2 Pears, peeled and chopped
- 1.5 cups chilled almond milk
- 3 medjool dates, pitted
- 1 tablespoon almond butter
- 1 tablespoon cacao
- 1 tablespoon chia seeds
- 3-4 ice cubes

Method:

Add all ingredients to blender. Blend on high speed. Serve immediately.

Avocado and Bacon Brekkie Pizza

Prep: 5 Min   Cook: 15 Min   Serves: 4

Ingredients:

- 3 large avocados, halved, stone removed
- 2 teaspoons lemon juice
- salt and pepper
- 2 large Lebanese flatbreads
- 1 1/2 cups grated mozzarella
- 8 slices streaky bacon
- 400g truss cherry tomatoes
- 2 eggs
- 1 tablespoon olive oil
- micro sprouts and hot sauce, to serve

Method:

Preheat oven to 220°C fan forced. Place the avocado, lemon juice, salt and pepper in a medium bowl and crush with a fork until smooth

Spread each flatbread with the avocado mixture and sprinkle with cheese

Divide the bacon and the tomatoes between each pizza. Make a slight well in the centre of each flatbread and crack the egg into it. Season with salt and pepper and drizzle with a little oil

Cook for 13–15 minutes, or until the egg is just set and the bacon is cooked. Serve sprinkled with sprouts and with hot sauce

Weet-Bix Berry Smoothie

Prep: 5 Min   Serves: 2

Makes: Approx 1 Litre

Ingredients:

- 2 frozen bananas, chopped
- 4 Sanitarium Weet-Bix
- 1 1/2 cups soy milk
- 2 cup strawberries, hulled and washed
- 1 cup Greek yoghurt
- 3-4 medjool dates, seeds removed, roughly chopped

Method:

Place all ingredients into a blender. Blend on high speed until combined
Pour into serving glasses. Serve over ice, if desired

Egg and avocado flip over

Prep: 5 Minutes   Cook: 10 Minutes   Serves: 1

Ingredients:

- 3 eggs, lightly beaten
- 60ml (¼ cup) low fat milk
- 1/3 cup grated cheddar cheese
- 3 teaspoons olive oil
- 1/2 small avocado, diced
- 1 small tomato, thinly sliced
- 2 teaspoons lemon juice
- 1 tablespoon chopped fresh chives
- Basil, to serve

Method:

Preheat grill to high. Whisk eggs and milk in a medium bowl. Season with salt and pepper

Heat 2 tsp oil in a non-stick 20cm frying pan.

Pour in egg mixture and cook over medium heat for 3-4 minutes until almost set.

Sprinkle omelette with cheese and place under hot grill for a few minutes until puffed and golden

Toss avocado and tomato with lemon juice and remaining teaspoon of oil.

Sprinkle avocado mixture and half the herbs over one-half of omelette.

Fold omelette in half and slide onto a warm plate to serve. Scatter with remaining herbs

Green eggs & ham

Prep: 5 Min   Cook: 10 Min   Serves: 4

Ingredients:

- 8 eggs
- 2 teaspoons olive oil
- 25g (1/3 cup) grated parmesan cheese
- 120g baby spinach
- 4 seeded brioche buns, split, toasted
- 80g thinly sliced lean leg ham

Method:

Place eggs, 100g spinach and parmesan into a blender and blend until combined.
Season with salt and pepper.
Heat a large non-stick frying pan over medium heat until hot. Add the oil and swirl to coat pan base.
Add egg mixture and cook for 1½ minutes or until mixture starts to set. Using a spatula, push set egg towards centre of pan, tilting pan to allow uncooked egg to run over base.
Cook for 2 minutes or until eggs form creamy curds.
Top bun base with spinach leaves, ham and green eggs.
Sprinkle with parmesan, top with bun lids to serve.

Mexican Sweet Potato Family Hash Brown

Prep: 15 Minutes   Cook: 20 Minutes   Serves: 4-6

Ingredients:

- 8 eggs
- ¼ cup (60ml) milk
- 1 tbsp taco seasoning mix
- 2 cloves garlic, crushed
- 3 cups (approx. 500g) grated and firmly packed sweet potato
- 2 cups (200g) shredded tasty cheese
- 2 green onions, finely sliced
- ⅓ cup finely chopped coriander leaves, plus extra for garnish
- Salt and pepper, to taste
- 1 tbsp olive oil
- Guacamole and hot sauce, to serve

Method:

Preheat oven to 180°C/160°C (fan-forced)
Whisk 4 eggs, milk, seasoning and garlic in a large bowl. Add sweet potato, 1 ½ cups cheese, green onions and coriander. Mix well. Season with salt and pepper
Heat the oil in a large ovenproof frying pan (20cm base/26cm top) over a medium heat, swirling to coat base and sides of pan. Add sweet potato mixture. Flatten top and cook for about 5 minutes or until base is golden
Form four indents in mixture with the back of a spoon. Scatter with remaining cheese. Crack an egg into each hole. Cook in oven for 15 minutes, or until hash brown is firm to touch and egg whites are set
Serve with guacamole and hot sauce. Garnish with extra coriander leaves

Huevos Rancheros (Mexican baked eggs)

Prep: 15 Minutes   Cook: 30-35 Minutes   Serves: 4

Ingredients:

- 2 tablespoons olive oil
- 1 brown onion, finely chopped
- ½ teaspoon chilli flakes
- 1 teaspoon smoked paprika
- 2 teaspoons ground cumin
- Salt and pepper, to season
- 1 large (300g) red capsicum, deseeded, finely chopped
- 400g kidney beans, drained, rinsed
- 400g can diced tomatoes
- ½ cup (125ml) water
- 4 eggs, at room temperature
- ½ cup coriander leaves
- 1 avocado, thinly sliced
- Sour cream, lime wedges and small toasted tortillas, to serve

Method:

Preheat oven to 180°C (160°C fan forced). Heat oil in a large non-stick frying pan over medium heat. Add onion, chilli, smoked paprika, cumin, salt and pepper and cook for 4-5 minutes, or until softened. Add capsicum, kidney beans, tomatoes and water and bring to the boil. Reduce heat to a simmer and cook, stirring occasionally, for 8-10 minutes, or until thickened.

Spoon the mixture into four 1 cup-capacity ovenproof dishes. Make an indentation into each bean mixture, and crack an egg into each.

Bake for 15-18 minutes or until the egg is cooked to your liking. Serve your Mexican Eggs with coriander, avocado, sour cream, lime and tortillas.

Egg Cups with Bacon Dippers

Prep: 10 Minutes   Cook: 20 Minutes   Serves: 6

Ingredients:

- 50g butter, melted
- 6 slices Helga's Traditional Wholemeal bread, crusts removed and reserved
- 6 rashers streaky bacon, cut in half lengthways
- 40g baby spinach
- 1/3 cup shredded tasty cheese
- 6 eggs
- Chives, snipped, to serve

Method:

Preheat oven to 190°C. Brush a 6 hole muffin tin with half the melted butter for the egg cups. Grease and line a baking tray for the bacon dippers

Gently roll each slice of bread flat with a rolling pin and press each slice of bread into the prepared muffin hole. Brush with remaining melted butter

Wrap a strip of bacon around each reserved crust and place on the lined baking tray. Bake both trays in the oven for 10 minutes

Remove both from the oven, turn the bacon soldiers over. Place a few spinach leaves into the bread cups, and divide the cheese evenly between them. Gently crack an egg into each cup

Carefully place both trays back in the oven and bake for another 15 minutes or until the egg is just set and the bacon soldiers are crispy

Remove from the oven, allow cups to cool in pan for 5 minutes before removing. Serve sprinkled with chives, salt and pepper

Dip bacon soldiers into gooey eggs and enjoy!

Cheesy Bacon and Mushroom Bread Bake

Prep: 15 Min + 5 Min Cooling Time   Serves: 6

Cook: 1 Hr 10 Min

Ingredients:
- 6 rashes streaky bacon, coarsely chopped
- 400 g brown mushrooms, thickly sliced
- 1 cup (60 g) baby spinach leaves
- 2 spring onions, thinly sliced
- 12 eggs
- 600 ml thickened cream
- 1 cup (250 ml) milk
- 50 g (½ cup) Perfect Italiano™ Parmesan Grated
- 2 cloves garlic, crushed
- 225 g loaf sourdough, thickly sliced
- 2 cups (180 g) Perfect Italiano™ 4 Cheese Melt

Method:

Preheat oven to 200°C / 180°C fan-forced. Grease a deep 26cm (8 cup capacity) round ovenproof dish. Place on an oven tray

Heat a large non-stick fry pan over medium - high heat. Add bacon and cook for 3 minutes until browned. Add mushroom and cook, stirring for 5 minutes or until mushrooms are just tender. Stir in spinach and spring onions and cook for 1 minute or until spinach wilts. Remove from heat

Whisk together eggs, cream, milk, parmesan and garlic in a large jug. Pour egg mixture into prepared dish. Add cooked bacon mixture and stir to distribute. Arrange bread, upright, in prepared egg mixture. Sprinkle with 4 Cheese Melt and let stand for 10 minutes

Bake for 55 minutes or until golden brown and just set in the centre. Remove from oven. Stand for 5 minutes before serving

Waffles with Sauteed Mushrooms and Maple Bacon

Prep: 10 Mins   Cook: 15 Mins   Serves: 4

Ingredients:

- 8 (200g) rashers streaky bacon
- 1/4 cup maple syrup
- 1 egg, separated
- 1 tbsp caster sugar
- 3/4 cup (175ml) milk
- 80g butter, melted
- 1 cup (140g) self-raising flour
- 400g Swiss Brown Mushrooms, halved
- 2 tbsp chives, sliced
- Sour cream and chives to serve

Method:

Preheat oven to 180°C fan-forced. Line a baking tray with baking paper Place bacon in a single layer and brush with maple syrup. Cook for 20 minutes or until crisp

Place egg yolk, milk, 60g melted butter and flour together in a medium bowl and whisk to combine. Whisk egg whites and sugar in a small bowl until light and fluffy and gently fold into flour mixture

Preheat a waffle iron. Use 1/4 cup of the waffle batter at a time. Cook for 4 minutes or until golden

Melt remaining butter in a large frying pan over medium high heat. Add mushrooms and chives. Season with salt and pepper. Cook, stirring occasionally for about 5 minutes or until mushrooms are lightly golden

Place waffles on serving plates. Top with Maple Bacon, Mushrooms, sour cream and chives

Smoked Salmon and Dill Dutch Baby

Prep: 5 Minutes   Cook: 20 Minutes   Serves: 4

Ingredients:

PICKLED ONION

- ¼ cup (60ml) apple cider vinegar
- 2 tbsp caster sugar
- 2 tsp salt
- ⅓ cup (80ml) water
- 1 red onion, halved and sliced thinly

CRÈME FRAICHE TOPPING

- ½ cup (125ml) crème fraiche (or sour cream)
- 1 tsp lemon zest
- Salt and pepper

DUTCH BABY PANCAKE

- ⅔ cup (100g) plain flour
- 1 tsp salt
- ⅔ cup (160ml) milk
- 3 eggs
- 30g butter, diced

TO SERVE

- 150g smoked salmon slices
- Lemon wedges and extra dill fronds

Method:

PICKLED ONION
Combine vinegar, sugar, salt and water. Mix until sugar has dissolved. Add onion and toss to coat. Stand for 10 minutes. Drain just before serving

DUTCH BABY PANCAKE
Arrange one oven rack in the middle position and remove all other racks above or below. Set oven to 240°C/220°C (fan-forced) and place a 25cm (top measurement) ovenproof frying pan into oven to heat up

Combine flour and salt in a large mixing bowl and make a well in the centre. Pour in milk and add eggs. Whisk to a smooth batter and let rest for 10 minutes

Once oven has reached temperature, quickly remove hot frying pan from oven using oven mitts. Add butter and swirl pan to coat all the base and sides. Pour in batter and return to oven. Cook 15-18 minutes or until pancake has puffed up and sides are golden

CRÈME FRAICHE TOPPING
While pancake is cooking, mix together the crème fraiche and lemon zest. Season with salt and pepper. Refrigerate

TO SERVE
Remove from oven and top with dollops of crème fraiche, smoked salmon and pickled onion. Garnish with dill fronds. Cut into wedges and serve with extra dill and lemon wedges

Breakfast Chilaquiles Verde

Prep: 10 Mins   Cook: 15 Mins   Serves: 2

Ingredients:

- 1/2 cup store bought Green Tomato Pickle
- 1/2 cup Chipotle and Black Bean Salsa
- 1/2 packet Cobs Sea Salt Corn Chips
- Juice of 1 lime or 1 tablespoon
- 1 x 400g can chickpeas, drained and rinsed
- 100g feta, crumbled
- 2 eggs
- To serve, fresh avocado, diced tomato salsa

Method:

Preheat oven to 200°C
In a medium bowl, combine tomato pickle and chipotle bean salsa
In an oven proof 30cm frypan, stir in combined sauces over medium to medium high heat. Once bubbling, take off heat, add the chips, then scatter chickpeas and feta
Bake for 10 mins, or until hot and cheese has slightly softened
Meanwhile, in a non-stick fry pan, fry two eggs until cooked, but still runny
Remove pan from oven and top with the fried eggs, avocado and fresh salsa

Tips & Hints:
Green Tomato Pickle and Chipotle & Black Bean Salsa available at most supermarkets. Make your own tomato salsa by combining finely chopped Spanish (red) onion, tomatoes and parsley.

Cheesy Breakfast Strata with Roast Cherry Tomatoes

Prep: 15 Min (Plus 2 Hrs Chilling Time)   Cook: 40 Minutes

Serves: 4

Ingredients:

- 8 thick slices (680g) crunchy Italian bread (ciabatta), cut into triangles
- 30g unsalted butter
- 1 brown onion, finely chopped
- 4 cups baby spinach leaves
- Salt and pepper
- 8 eggs
- 2 cups milk
- 1½ cups (180g) grated vintage cheddar
- 200g vine-ripened cherry tomatoes
- Basil leaves, to serve

Method:

Arrange bread in a lightly greased 28cm x 16cm (3 litre-capacity) baking dish.
Heat butter in a large non-stick frying pan over medium heat.
Add onion and cook stirring for 4-5 minutes or until softened. Add spinach, salt and pepper and cook for 1 minute, until wilted.
Spoon over the bread, set aside.
Beat together 4 of the eggs, the milk and cheese.
Pour over the bread mixture.
Cover and refrigerate for at least 2 hours (or overnight) to soak.
Stand the strata at room temperature while the oven is preheating to 180°C fan forced. Using a large metal spoon, make 4 indentations into the bread mixture.
Crack the one of the remaining eggs into each indentation.
Cook for 20–25 minutes or until golden and eggs are cooked to your liking.
Place the tomatoes on an oven tray and roast for 10 minutes.
Serve the strata with tomatoes and basil leaves.

Family Breakfast Tart

Prep: 15 Minutes   Cook: 30 Minutes   Serves: 4

Ingredients:

CHEESY SAUCE

- 2 tbsp (40g) butter
- 2 tbsp plain flour
- ¾ cup (185ml) milk
- Salt to taste
- ½ cup (50g) pizza blend cheese

BREAKFAST TART

- 1 tbsp olive oil
- 100g sliced button mushrooms
- 1 small clove garlic, crushed
- Salt and pepper
- ¼ cup pesto (65g) plus extra to serve
- 1 sheets puff pastry, just thawed
- 4 small eggs

Method:

CHEESY SAUCE

Melt butter in a medium saucepan over medium heat and stir in flour. Cook for 1 minute

Pour in the milk in two batches, stirring well between each addition. Continue to stir until there are no lumps, about 5 minutes. Remove from heat and stir in salt and cheese. Set aside

BREAKFAST TART

Preheat oven to 220°C/200°C (fan-forced). Line a baking tray with baking paper

Working inside the pastry square, score a smaller square approx. 1-1 ½ cm from the edge. Prick middle of pastry several times with a fork. Bake 10 minutes. Pastry should have browned and puffed up

Push down cooked pastry centre and spoon over cheesy sauce leaving the pastry border free. Dollop over pesto and arrange mushrooms over the top, leaving room for the eggs to nest in

Crack an egg into each space and season with salt and pepper. Bake 10-12 minutes or until eggs white are cooked and yolks still runny

Stand for 5 minutes. Cut into 4 large squares, serve warm

Tray Bake Pancake with Raspberry and Mango

Prep: 10 Minutes   Cook: 25 Minutes   Serves: 4

Ingredients:

- 1 ⅔ cups (250g) plain flour
- 2 ½ tsp baking powder
- ¼ cup (55g) caster sugar
- 1 ¼ cups (310ml) milk
- 2 eggs
- 60g butter, melted and cooled
- 1 x 125g punnet fresh raspberries
- 1 fresh mango, peeled and sliced thinly
- ¼ cup (10g) toasted coconut chips for garnish
- Coconut yoghurt and maple syrup, to serve

Method:

Preheat oven to 200°C/180°C (fan-forced) and grease and line a 35cm x 25cm (base measurement) baking dish with baking paper

Sift flour and baking powder into a mixing bowl and add sugar. Make a well in the centre

Whisk milk and eggs together and add to flour; mix well. Stir in all but 1 tbsp of the melted butter. Pour into prepared tin

Arrange raspberries and mango slices over the top and brush with reserved melted butter. Bake 25 minutes. Cool slightly

To serve, cut into 12 squares. Stack 3 per serve and top with coconut chips, yoghurt, and a drizzle of maple syrup

Tips & Hints:

Use any fresh or frozen berries and mango. If using frozen, defrost before using.
Make batter the night before. Cover and refrigerate. When ready to cook, add toppings and bake. It may increase cook time by 5 minutes.
Refrigerate baked pancakes in a sealed container for 2-3 days. Warm before serving.
Other topping suggestions - raspberry and white chocolate; ricotta and fig.

Fluffy Japanese Pancakes

Prep: 15 Minutes Cook: 25 Minutes Serves: 2

Ingredients:

- 3 eggs
- 1 tbsp milk
- 1 tsp vanilla extract
- ¼ cup (35g) plain flour
- 1 tsp baking powder
- ½ tsp cream of tartar
- ¼ cup (55g) caster sugar
- Vegetable oil for greasing
- Water for steaming
- Icing sugar, maple syrup and berries, to serve

Method:

Separate eggs and place egg whites into a large mixing bowl. Chill in refrigerator for as long as possible

Meanwhile, whisk egg yolks, milk and vanilla together until thick and frothy. Sift in flour and baking powder and whisk until it forms a thick batter. Set aside

Place egg whites and cream of tartar into the bowl of an electric mixer and whisk on medium speed until frothy and eggs turn a pale colour

Gradually add sugar, a little at a time until egg whites become firm, glossy and forms stiff peaks

Whisk ⅓ of the egg whites into the egg yolk mixture and mix well to loosen batter. Add remaining egg white in two batches, whisking gently to avoid over beating. Batter should be thick and airy

Heat frying pan on the smallest hob over low heat for 10 minutes. This is to saturate the frying pan with even heat

RING METHOD: Brush pan and the inside of three (7cm diameter x 5cm high) metal rings with vegetable oil. Rub off excess with paper towel

Cooking with 2 or 3 rings at a time, spoon approx. ⅓ cup of batter into each ring. Cover with lid and set timer to 2 minutes. Uncover and add 2 tsp of water into the empty spaces of the pan. Recover and cook for a further 3 minutes or until bubbles start to appear on the top

Using an offset spatula or egg flip, turn pancakes over and add another 2 tsp of water to pan. Cover again and cook a further 2-3 minutes, until mixture just starts pulling away from the side of ring. Remove and transfer to serving plate and remove rings. Repeat with remaining batter

ICE CREAM SCOOP METHOD: Brush heated pan with oil and wipe off excess with paper towel. Spoon a large ice cream scoop of batter into pan. Flatten top. Cover and cook for 2 minutes. Add another smaller scoop on top. Cover again and cook for 2 minutes. Turn over and cover to finish cooking, approx. 2 minutes. Repeat with remaining batter

Serve immediately dusted with icing sugar, maple syrup and berries

Nectarine and apricot coconut chia puddings

Prep: 25 Min   Cook: 1 Hr Setting Time   Serves: 4

Ingredients:

- 2 x 270m cans coconut milk
- 3/4 cup white chia seeds
- 1 teaspoon vanilla extract
- 4 yellow nectarines, stone removed, cut into thin wedges
- 4 apricots, stone removed, finely diced
- 1/2 cup maple syrup, to serve
- ¼ cup toasted flaked coconut, to serve
- *Email shopping list to:

Method:

Place coconut milk, chia seeds and vanilla into a bowl and stir until well combined. Set aside for 15 minutes to thicken.

Spoon half the chia mixture into the base of 4x 1 cup capacity glasses or glass bowls. Top with half the peaches and apricots. Spoon remaining chia seed mixture over fruit. Place remaining fruit onto chia seed mixture. Place in refrigerator for 1 hour or until cold. Drizzle maple syrup over fruit. Sprinkle with coconut and serve.

Coconut Raspberry Pancakes

Prep: 5 Minutes   Cook: 35 Minutes   Makes: 12

Ingredients:

- 2 cups self-raising flour
- 1/2 cup caster sugar
- 1 1/2 cups coconut milk
- 2 eggs
- Coconut oil or spray
- 2 tablespoons IXL Raspberry jam, warmed
- Berries and jam to serve

Method:

Pre-heat oven to 100°C. Line a tray with baking paper
Sift flour into a bowl. Stir in sugar. Combine coconut milk and eggs in a jug, whisk
Make a well in the centre of the flour and sugar, whisk in combined coconut milk and eggs, until a smooth batter forms. Stir in warmed jam. Set batter aside for 10 minutes
Heat a non-stick frying pan over medium high heat. Brush or spray with coconut oil. Spoon a 1/4 cup of mixture for each pancake into the pan. Cook for 2 minutes or until bubbles surface, flip and cook other side for minute
Transfer to the oven to keep warm, repeat with remaining pancakes
Serve with extra warmed jam and berries

Tips & Hints:
Top with toasted shredded coconut, and dollop with yoghurt.

Strawberry Swirl Yoghurt & Banana Sundaes

Prep: 15 Mins   Makes: 4

Ingredients:

- 375g strawberries, hulled
- 1 tbs caster sugar
- 2 cups reduced fat thick Greek-style yoghurt
- 2 ripe bananas
- ¾ cup granola or toasted muesli

Method:

Place 250g strawberries and sugar into a high-powered blender. Blend, stirring if necessary, until roughly pureed. Place yoghurt into a bowl. Swirl the pureed strawberries through yoghurt.

Peel and slice bananas. Slice remaining strawberries. Layer strawberry yoghurt, granola or toasted muesli, bananas and strawberries in serving glasses and serve.

Berry Nice Weet-Bix Breakfast in a Jar

Prep: 10 Minutes   Serves: 4

Ingredients:

- 8 Sanitarium Weet-Bix
- 2 cups frozen blueberries
- 2 cups natural yoghurt
- 4 kiwi fruits, diced
- 1/4 cup toasted flaked almonds

Method:

Using a small saucepan, warm the blueberries until just defrosted and producing small amount of juice but still keeping their shape

Roughly break-up Weet-Bix and add to each glass
Divide berries in each jar then top with yoghurt

Add kiwi fruit then fill jars with another layer of Weet-Bix, berries and yoghurt
Top with flaked almonds

Cinnamon French Toast Muffins

Prep: 10 Min   Cook: 25 Min   Makes: 12 Muffins

Ingredients:

- 6 large eggs
- 2 cups milk
- 2 teaspoons cinnamon
- 1 tablespoon brown sugar
- 1 tablespoon vanilla essence
- 1 loaf Helga's Traditional White Bread, cut into 1cm cubes

Method:

Preheat oven to 180°C. Grease a 12-hole muffin tin

In a large bowl, whisk eggs, milk, cinnamon, sugar and vanilla. Add cubed bread and use clean hands to gently toss and evenly coat all of the bread pieces

Set aside for 5 minutes to allow for the bread to absorb the liquid

Gently stir one last time, then divide mix between muffin holes, pressing gently to make compact and to use up all of the bread

Bake for 25 minutes or until cooked. Cool in muffin tin for 5 minutes before scooping out

Brush or drizzle with maple syrup

The Ultimate Ham, Cheese and Spinach Breakfast Loaf

Prep: 20 Minutes   Cook: 10 Minutes   Makes: 1 Large Loaf

Ingredients:

CHEESE BECHAMEL SAUCE

- 1 cup Devondale Full Cream Milk, heated
- 25g Devondale Original Butter
- 2 tbsp plain flour
- 1/2 cup Devondale 3 Cheese Blend
- 1 tablespoon Dijon Mustard
- Salt and pepper, to taste

LOAF

- 1 sourdough bread loaf
- 1/2 cup Dijon mustard
- 250g shaved deli ham
- 1 cup baby spinach
- 1 1/2 cups Devondale 3 Cheese Blend

Method:

CHEESE BECHAMEL SAUCE

Melt butter in a saucepan over medium heat. Slowly add the flour, until combined

Add milk and whisk constantly until the sauce is well combined. Cook and continue to stir for another 5 minutes until the sauce is thick and glossy and coats the back of a wooden spoon

Stir through the cheese and mustard. Season to taste. Transfer to a bowl

LOAF

Preheat the oven to 200°C (180°C fan forced). Slice off the top crust layer of the loaf. Place the loaf on it's side and cut lengthways down the centre of the loaf

Spread the bottom side of the loaf with Dijon mustard. Top with a layer of ham slices, and a layer of spinach leaves. Drizzle over 1/2 of the bechamel sauce and top with 1/2 of the cheese

Place the top on the loaf. Transfer to a baking paper covered tray. Spread remaining bechamel sauce on the top layer of the loaf. Sprinkle over cheese and transfer to the oven for 10-15 minutes or until cheese is golden and loaf is toasted

Slice the loaf in triangles and serv

Ham, cranberry and camembert French toasts

Prep: 10 Minutes   Cook: 15 Minutes   Serves: 4

Ingredients:

- 4 eggs, at room temperature
- ¾ cup milk
- 25g (1/3 cup) finely grated parmesan cheese
- Salt and pepper
- 8 slices sourdough bread
- ¼ cup (80g) cranberry jelly
- 4 slices (60g each) leftover Christmas ham
- 150g leftover camembert, sliced
- 2 tablespoons seeded mustard
- Butter, for greasing
- Extra seeded mustard, to serve
- Cornichons, to serve

Method:

Preheat oven to 120°C fan forced. Whisk eggs, milk, parmesan, salt and pepper together in a shallow dish.
Spread one side of half the bread slices with cranberry jelly and top with ham and camembert. Spread remaining bread with mustard and sandwich together.
Grease a large non-stick frying pan with butter and melt over medium heat. Dip 2 sandwiches into the egg mixture for about 15 seconds each side.
Add to pan and cook for 2-3 minutes each side or until golden brown. Transfer to an oven tray in the oven to keep warm. Repeat with remaining butter, egg mixture and sandwiches.
Slice French toast in half and serve with extra mustard and cornichons.

Garlic Mushroom and Chives Dutch Baby

Prep: 10 Minutes   Cook: 20 Minutes   Serves: 4

Ingredients:

DUTCH BABY PANCAKE
- ⅔ cup (100g) plain flour
- 1 tsp salt
- ⅔ cup (160ml) milk
- 3 eggs
- 30g butter, diced

GARLIC MUSHROOMS
- 2 tbsp olive oil
- 40g butter, diced
- 300g Swiss brown mushrooms, halved
- 3 cloves garlic, crushed
- Salt and pepper

TO SERVE
- 3 tbsp chopped chives
- ⅓ cup marinated goats curd
- Fresh thyme sprigs for garnish (optional)

Method:

DUTCH BABY PANCAKE
Arrange one oven rack in the middle position and remove all other racks above or below. Set oven to 240°C/220°C (fan-forced) and place a 25 cm (top measurement) ovenproof frying pan into oven to heat up
Combine flour and salt in a large mixing bowl and make a well in the centre. Pour in milk and add eggs. Whisk to a smooth batter and let rest for 10 minutes
Once oven has reached temperature, quickly remove hot frying pan from oven using oven mitts. Add butter and swirl pan to coat all the base and sides. Pour in batter and return to oven. Cook 15-18 minutes or until pancake has puffed up and sides are golden

GARLIC MUSHROOMS
While pancake is cooking, heat oil and butter in a frying pan over medium-high heat. Add mushrooms and cook stirring for 5-6 minutes. Stir in garlic and season with salt and pepper, cook a further few minutes. Remove and set aside

TO SERVE
Remove frying pan from oven and immediately top with garlic mushrooms, chopped chives and dollops of marinated goats curd. Garnish with fresh thyme sprigs and cut into wedges. Serve immediately

Kedgeree

Prep: 10 Minutes   Cook: 20 Minutes   Serves: 4

Ingredients:

- 4 eggs
- 2 tbsp olive oil
- 1 large onion, finely chopped
- 2 cloves garlic, crushed
- 3 tsp mild curry powder
- 1 ½ cups (250g) basmati rice
- 650ml chicken stock
- Salt and pepper
- 1 cup (120g) frozen peas
- 150g hot smoked salmon, skin removed, flaked
- Chopped fresh parsley, to garnish
- Greek yoghurt and lemon wedges, to serve

Method:

Place eggs in a saucepan and cover with water. Bring to a gentle boil and cook for 5 minutes (medium boiled eggs), or until cooked to your liking. Drain and immerse in cold water. Peel and slice eggs in half

Meanwhile, heat oil in a large, non-stick frying pan over a medium heat. Add onion and garlic. Cook, stirring for 3 minutes, or until soft. Add curry powder. Cook, stirring for 1 minute, or until fragrant. Stir in rice

Add stock to pan and stir to combine. Simmer gently covered, for 10 minutes. Remove lid. Stir in peas. Cover and cook for a further 3 to 5 minutes, or until rice is tender and peas are cooked. Remove from the heat. Scatter over flaked salmon

Top with eggs. Garnish with chopped parsley. Serve with yoghurt and lemon wedges

Tips & Hints:

Replace salmon with flaked tuna or canned salmon.

Garnish with chopped green chilli or drizzle with green sriracha just before serving.

Replace chopped parsley with chopped coriander.

Kedgeree can be served warm or cold. Great for lunchboxes or picnics.

To increase the eggs in recipe, stir 3 chopped boiled eggs through rice with salmon and serve another 3 eggs halved on top.

Herbed mushroom waffle omelettes

Prep: 7 Minutes   Cook: 8 Minutes   Serves: 4

Ingredients:

- 200g button mushrooms, thinly sliced
- 5 eggs
- 3 tablespoons milk
- 2 tablespoons finely chopped fresh chives
- Baby herbs, to serve
- Grated parmesan, to serve

Method:

Preheat waffle maker. Wait for the green READY light to go on
Place mushroom slices in waffle maker. Cook for 2 minutes or until browned. Set aside a third of the mushrooms to serve
Meanwhile, whisk egg and milk together in a jug. Season with salt and pepper
Reheat waffle maker. Wait for the green READY light to go on. Scatter two thirds of the mushrooms and chives over base of waffle machine. Pour over egg mixture
Close lid and cook for 5 minutes or until set. Carefully remove waffle omelettes from waffle maker. Serve scattered with remaining mushrooms, chives, baby herbs and parmesan

Turkish Eggs with Yoghurt and Herb Salad

Prep: 15 Min   Cook: 5 Min   Serves: 4

Ingredients:

- Turkish bread, sliced
- 200g tub thick Greek-style yoghurt
- ¼ cup (60ml) olive oil
- 8 eggs
- 2 small avocados, cut into wedges
- 60g baby spinach
- 2 green onions, thinly sliced
- Fresh coriander, mint and dill leaves, to serve
- ½ teaspoon mild paprika
- ¼ teaspoon dried chilli flakes
- 100g feta cheese

Method:

Heat a large chargrill pan over high heat. Lightly spray both sides of bread with oil. Cook bread for 1-2 minutes on each side or until charred and warm

Heat half the oil in a non-stick frying pan over medium-high heat. Crack eggs one at a time into hot pan. Cook for 2 minutes, until whites are set and crispy around the edges

Spread yoghurt on a serving plate. Top with 2 eggs. Arrange avocado, spinach, green onion and herb leaves on plates

Add remaining oil to pan over medium heat. Add paprika and chilli. Cook for 30 seconds or until fragrant. Spoon oil over eggs. Crumble over the feta and serve with the Turkish toasts

Egg Florentine Breakfast Bake

Prep: 15 Minutes　　　　Cook: 40 Minutes　　　　Serves: 6-8

Ingredients:

- 1 tablespoon olive oil
- 1 brown onion, finely chopped
- 2 garlic cloves, crushed
- 250g button mushrooms, sliced
- 200g baby spinach leaves
- 10 eggs
- 125ml (1/2 cup) milk
- 40g (1/2 cup) grated parmesan cheese
- 200g grape tomatoes, halved
- Basil leaves, to serve

Method:

Preheat oven to 180°C/160°C fan-forced. Lightly spray a 20 x 30cm (base measurement) baking tin with oil and line with baking paper.

Heat oil in a large non-stick frying pan over medium-high heat. Cook onion, stirring, for 3-4 minutes or until softened. Add garlic and mushrooms and cook, stirring, for 3-4 minutes or until golden. Add spinach and stir until just wilted. Set aside to cool slightly.

Whisk eggs, milk and half the parmesan together in a large bowl. Season with salt and pepper. Spread mushroom mixture over base of prepared dish. Pour over egg mixture and evenly distribute vegetables. Top with halved cherry tomatoes cut side up and sprinkle with remaining parmesan.

Bake for 30 minutes or until golden and set. Let stand for 10 minutes. Serve warm or at room temperature scattered with basil.

Tips & Hints:
Note: You can do this in a baking tin or a baking dish (1.5 litre/ 6-cup). Cooking time will increase slightly in a baking dish.

Egg and Prosciutto Breakfast Pizza

Prep: 15 Mins   Cook: 10 Mins   Makes: 2 Pizzas

Ingredients:

PIZZA DOUGH

- 1 ¼ cups warm water
- 3 teaspoons instant dried yeast
- 1 teaspoon caster sugar
- 1 teaspoon sea salt flakes
- 1 tablespoon olive oil
- 3 cups plain flour

PIZZA TOPPING

- 1/2 cup tomato passata
- 1 1/2 cups shredded pizza cheese
- 100g shaved prosciutto
- 30g baby spinach leaves, plus extra to serve
- 8 eggs
- 1/2 cup finely grated parmesan
- Basil leaves, to serve

Method:

PIZZA DOUGH

Preheat oven to 240°C/220°C fan forced. Line 2 large baking trays with baking paper

To make the pizza dough, whisk water, yeast, sugar, salt and olive oil in a jug. Stand in a warm place for 10 minutes or until frothy. Put flour into a large bowl. Add yeast mixture and stir until a soft dough forms. Turn onto a floured surface and knead for 5 minutes or until smooth

Divide dough in half and roll each half out on a floured surface to make two 26cm rounds. Transfer to prepared trays

PIZZA TOPPING

Spread pizza bases with passata, sprinkle with pizza cheese and spinach leaves. Arrange 4 prosciutto slices on top of each base to make little nests. Gently crack eggs into prosciutto nests and sprinkle with parmesan. Bake for 12-15 minutes or until golden and cooked through

Serve pizzas scattered with basil and extra spinach leaves

Avo Green Smoothie

Prep: 5 Minutes   Serves: 4

Ingredients:

- 1 avocado, peeled and deseeded
- 60g baby spinach
- 1 Lebanese cucumber, roughly chopped
- 1 banana
- 400ml milk
- 1 lemon, zested, peeled and finely chopped
- 1/2 cup Chobani natural yoghurt
- 1 cup ice
- *Email shopping list to:

Method:

Place all ingredients in a blender and blend until smooth

Pour mixture evenly into 3 glasses and sprinkle with lemon zest

Egg Tacos

Prep: 15 Mins   Cook: 10 Mins   Serves: 4

Ingredients

- 6 eggs
- 1/2 cup light cooking cream
- 1 tablespoon olive oil
- 1 small red onion, finely diced
- 1/4 cup finely diced green capsicum
- 2 small tomatoes, seeds removed, finely diced
- 8 mini stand 'n' stuff taco shells
- 8 small baby cos lettuce leaves
- 1 avocado, finely diced
- 1/4 cup light sour cream
- 1/4 cup grated tasty cheese

Method:

1. Break eggs into a bowl. Add cream, salt and white pepper. Set aside
2. Heat oil in a non-stick frying pan over medium heat. Add onion and capsicum and cook for 3 minutes or until softened. Stir through tomato. Add egg mixture and cook for 2 minutes or until beginning to set. Gently stir. Cook for 1 minute and stir again or until egg is just set
3. Meanwhile, heat taco shells following packet directions
4. Place warmed taco shells onto a platter. Fill with lettuce, egg mixture, diced avocado, sour cream and cheese

Tips & Hints:

You can swap out the taco shells for soft-shell tacos or burrito wraps. For a lighter lower-carb version, simply serve in large cos lettuce cups.

Ricotta, Leek and Corn Fritters with Zucchini Noodles

Prep: 5 Mins   Cook: 10 Mins   Serves: 4

Ingredients:

- 400g Perfect Italiano Ricotta
- 40g Perfect Italiano Parmesan, grated
- 1 leek, sliced
- 1 can sweet corn kernels
- 80g flour
- 4 eggs
- 1 tbsp. olive oil
- 2 large zucchinis, finely sliced or noodled
- 1 red chili, finely sliced
- 1 lemon, juiced

Method:

1. In a bowl combine the Ricotta and Parmesan, leeks, corn kernels, flour, eggs and a pinch of salt and pepper. Shape batter into fritters
2. Heat a non-stick pan, add olive oil and cook each fritter until golden brown and cooked through
3. Whilst fritters are cooking put the zucchini though the spiralise machine (alternatively finely slice) then toss with chili, lemon juice, olive oil and salt pepper
4. Serve fritters with zucchini noodles

Fun Brekky Eggs in Toast

Prep: 5 Minutes   Cook: 5 Minutes   Serves: 2

Ingredients:

- 2 thick slices wholemeal bread
- Butter or margarine, for spreading
- 2 tsp olive oil
- 2 eggs, at room temperature
- 1/4 cup finely grated reduced fat tasty cheese

Method:

1. Place bread onto a board. Lightly spread both sides with butter or margarine. Using a cookie cutter, cut a fun shape out of the centre of each slice of bread
2. Heat oil in a large non-stick frying pan. Add bread and cut-out shapes. Cook for 2-3 minutes until golden. Turn bread and crack an egg into the centre of each slice. Cook for 3-4 minutes until egg yolk is almost set
3. Sprinkle with cheese and heat until just melting. Serve each with matching cut-out shapes

Tips & Hints:

Tip: Get the kids involved by using their favourite cookie cutter shapes

Nut and Cacao Smoothie

Prep: 5 Minutes Serves: 1

Ingredients:

- 1 cup chilled milk
- 1 tablespoon cacoa powder
- 1 small ripe banana, peeled
- 1/4 small ripe avocado, flesh removed
- 1 tablespoon
- Handful of ice-cubes

Method:

Place all ingredients into a blender.

Blend until smooth and serve.

Eggspert Eggs on Sauteed Greens with Pancetta and Pine Nuts

Prep: 10 Minutes   Cook: 15 Minutes   Serves: 4

Ingredients:

- 4 x 60g eggs
- 8 thin slices (80g) pancetta
- 2 bunches (150g each) asparagus, woody ends trimmed
- 20g butter
- 1 leek, trimmed, thinly sliced crosswise (white and pale green parts only)
- 2 cloves garlic, crushed
- Zest of 1 lemon
- 1 cup (140g) frozen peas, thawed
- Salt and black pepper
- 1 tablespoon toasted pine nuts

Method:

1. Put eggs on the egg tray and lower into the pot of the Egg Poacher. Fill with water up to the EGGSPERT fill line. Cover with the lid and insert probe through the vent. Press METHOD button to select EGGSPERT. The default temperature and time are shown on the LCD screen. Press START
2. Meanwhile, in a large non-stick pan, saute pancetta, turning once, over medium-low heat, until crisp and lightly brown. Take out and set aside. In the same frying pan fry asparagus for 1-2 minutes until bright green and tender crisp. Set aside
3. Add butter to pan. Add leek and saute, on medium heat, for 3-4 minutes or until softened
4. Add garlic, lemon zest and peas and cook for about 1 minute, or until fragrant, season
5. When the Eggspert eggs have finished cooking, take them out and run under cold water. Use the egg topper to top the eggs and pour eggs out onto a plate
6. Serve greens with pancetta topped with an Eggspert egg. Sprinkle with pine nuts and black pepper

Avocado on toast: 2 ways

Prep: 5 Min Each VarietyServes: 6

Ingredients:

AVOCADO AND BACON

- Half avocado
- 2 rashers crisp chopped bacon
- 1/4 tsp chilli flakes
- 1 tsp aioli

AVOCADO AND FETA

- Half avocado, smashed
- Crumbled feta
- 1 tbsp pomegranate seeds
- Chopped almonds

Method:

AVOCADO AND BACON

On top of sourdough place fanned sliced avocado and top with crisp chopped bacon, chilli flakes and aioli

AVOCADO AND FETA

On top of sourdough placed smashed avocado, crumbled feta, pomegranate seeds and serve with chopped almonds

Weet-Bix Breakfast Cookies

Prep: 10 Min   Cook: 12 Min   Makes: 12 Biscuits

Ingredients:

- 4 Sanitarium Weet-Bix, crushed
- 1 cup plain flour, sifted
- 1/2 teaspoon bi-carb soda
- 1 teaspoon cinnamon
- 3/4 cup margarine
- 1 teaspoon vanilla essence
- 4 medjool dates, seeds removed and roughly chopped
- 1 large apple, coarsely grated
- 1/2 cup craisins, or sultanas
- 1 egg, lightly beaten
- 2 tablespoons maple syrup

Method:

1. Preheat oven to 180°C
2. Combine Weet-Bix, flour, bi-carb soda and cinnamon in a medium bowl
3. In a separate bowl, combine margarine and vanilla essence
4. Add dry mix into margarine mix and stir to combine. Then add the remaining ingredients
5. Using 1/4 cup measurements, roll mixture into small balls and place onto a lined baking tray. Lightly press each ball and bake for 20 minutes or until cooked
6. Cool on the baking tray for 5 minutes, then transfer to a wire rack to cool completely

Vegetable Fritters with Poached Egg

Prep: 15 Mins   Cook: 20 Mins   Makes: 12   Serves: 4

Ingredients:

- 2 large zucchini, trimmed, sliced
- 2 cups (about 300g) diced pumpkin
- 1 carrot, trimmed, sliced
- 1 cup mint leaves
- 3 green onions, thinly sliced
- 1/2 cup frozen peas, thawed
- 1 1/2 cups panko breadcrumbs
- 1/2 cup self-raising flour
- 150g feta cheese, crumbled
- 5 eggs
- 1/3 cup olive oil

Method:

1. Preheat oven to 180°C. Line a baking tray with baking paper. Place zucchini in a food processor and process until finely chopped. Transfer to a clean kitchen cloth and squeeze, over a bowl or the sink, to remove excess liquid. (This prevents the fritters from being soggy). Place zucchini in a large bowl
2. Add pumpkin, carrot and mint to food processor and process until finely chopped. Add to zucchini with onion, peas, breadcrumbs, flour and feta. Lightly whisk 1 egg in a small bowl and add to vegetable mixture. Season. Stir until combined. Form 1/3 cups of the veggie mixture into fritters and place on a tray
3. Heat half the oil in a non-stick frying pan over medium heat. Cook fritters in batches, adding more if needed, for 3 minutes each side or until golden. Transfer to prepared tray and place in oven to cook for 10 minutes or until cooked through
4. Meanwhile, bring a medium saucepan of water to the boil. Reduce heat to low, and when bubbles subside, use a spoon to stir the water until a whirlpool forms. Break an egg into a small bowl and gently slide into whirlpool. Cook for 3 minutes or until white is cooked. Use a slotted spoon to transfer egg to a plate. Repeat with remaining eggs

Tips & Hints:
You can make smaller, snack-sized fritters if you like, just use 2 tablespoonsful of the mixture for each. Fritters will keep for up to 3 days in an airtight container in the fridge.

Smoky Baked Beans with Poached Eggs

Prep: 20 Minutes   Cook: 30 Minutes   Serves: 4

Ingredients:

1. 1 tablespoons olive oil
2. 1 red onion, finely chopped
3. 3 celery sticks, diced
4. 100g smoked bacon, trimmed, diced
5. 2 garlic cloves, crushed
6. 3 teaspoons smoked paprika
7. 2 tablespoons tomato paste
8. 2 x 400g cans cannellini beans, rinsed, drained
9. 400g can diced tomatoes
10. 1 tablespoon Worcestershire sauce
11. 1 tablespoon pure maple syrup
12. 4 eggs
13. Fresh parsley sprigs, to serve
14. Toasted sourdough, to serve

Method:

1. Heat the oil in a large saucepan over medium heat. Cook onion, celery and bacon, stirring, for 6-7 minutes or until light golden. Add garlic and paprika and cook, stirring, for 1 minute or until fragrant. Add tomato paste and cook, stirring, for 1 minute.
2. Add beans, canned tomatoes, Worcestershire sauce, maple syrup and 80ml (1/3 cup) water and stir to combine. Bring to the boil. Reduce heat to low and simmer, uncovered, for 20 minutes or until thick.
3. Meanwhile, fill a large deep-frying pan three-quarters with water and bring to the boil. Reduce heat and keep at a simmer. Carefully break 1 egg into a cup and slide into water. Repeat with remaining eggs. Poach eggs gently for 1-2 minutes or until egg whites are set and yolks are still soft.
4. Serve beans topped with a poached egg and sprinkled with parsley.

Tips & Hints:
You can make the baked beans ahead and freeze them (without the egg). Place in airtight containers and freeze for up to 1 month.

Breakfast soft-shell tacos

Prep: 10 Minutes   Cook: 10 Minutes   Serves: 4

Ingredients:

- 8 eggs
- 80ml (1/3 cup) milk
- 2 teaspoons olive oil
- 80g feta cheese, crumbled
- 4 x 40g tortillas, chargrilled
- 110g (1/3 cup) tomato relish
- 2 tablespoons chopped fresh chives
- 2/3 cup mixed baby herbs

Method:

1. Whisk eggs and milk together in a large bowl. Season with salt and pepper.
2. Heat oil in a large non-stick frying pan over medium heat. Add egg mixture and cook for 1 1/2 minutes or until mixture starts to set. Using a spatula, push set egg towards centre of pan, tilting pan to allow uncooked egg to run over base. Cook for 2-3 minutes or until eggs form creamy curds. Stir in feta.
3. Divide eggs between wraps. Top with tomato relish, chives and herbs. Wrap to enclose filling.

Zucchini Fritters with Portabella Mushrooms and Poached Egg

Prep: 10 Mins   Cook: 15 Mins   Makes: 8 Fritters   Serves: 4

Ingredients:

- 4 (240g) Portabella Mushrooms, thickly sliced
- 50g butter
- 240g truss cherry tomatoes, cut into 4 lengths
- 1/3 cup olive oil
- 350g zucchini, grated
- 100g halloumi cheese, chopped
- 1 tsp sweet paprika
- 2 green onions, thinly sliced
- 6 eggs
- 1/2 cup (75g) self raising flour
- 1/3 cup (75ml) milk

Method:

1. Heat butter in a large saucepan over medium heat. Once melted, add mushrooms and cook for 5 minutes or until tender and lightly browned. Remove mushrooms and set aside
2. Meanwhile, preheat oven to 180°C fan forced. Line a baking tray with baking paper. Place cherry tomatoes on the baking tray and drizzle with 2 tablespoons olive oil. Season with salt and pepper. Cook for 10-12 minutes or until tomatoes have softened
3. Using hands squeeze zucchini to remove any excess liquid. Combine zucchini, halloumi, paprika and green onion in a medium bowl. Season with salt and pepper. Combine flour, 2 eggs and milk in a separate bowl. Add zucchini mixture and stir gently until combined
4. Heat 1/3 of the oil in a large frying pan over medium heat. Drop 1/4 cup of the fritter mixture into a pan and cook, in batches, for 5 minutes each side or until cooked through
5. Meanwhile, poach remaining 4 eggs in a pan of simmering water for 4-5 minutes or until cooked to your liking
6. Place zucchini fritters on plate, top with mushrooms, poached egg and cherry tomatoes to serve

Easy Fruit Pancakes

Prep: 20 Minutes   Cook: 25 Minutes   Makes: 12

Ingredients:

- 1 cup self-raising flour
- 1/2 tsp baking powder
- 1 cup reduced fat milk
- 1 egg
- 40g butter, melted
- 1 cup canned diced peaches, pears or apricots, well drained on paper towel and/or sliced ripe banana
- Icing sugar, for dusting

Method:

1. Sift flour and baking powder into a large bowl. Make a well in the centre. Whisk milk and egg in a jug then pour into the centre of flour mixture. Stir to form a smooth batter. Fold 2 tsp melted butter through mixture
2. Heat a medium non-stick frying pan over medium-low heat. Brush the base of the pan with melted butter. Spoon 1 1/2 tbs batter into the pan and spread to form a 10cm round pancake. Sprinkle with chopped fruit or a few slices of banana
3. Cook for 3 minutes until bubbles appear on the surface. Turn and cook further 3-4 minutes until cooked through. Transfer to a plate. Repeat, reheating the pan and brushing with butter between batches
4. Top extra fruit and vanilla yoghurt to serve if you like

Tips & Hints:
The baking power adds extra lightness to the cooked pancakes

Green Shakshuka

Prep: 15 Mins   Cook: 15 Mins   Serves: 6

Ingredients:

- 2 tablespoons olive oil
- 2 leeks, white part only, thinly sliced
- 1 large green capsicum, deseeded, diced
- 2 teaspoons ground cumin
- 1 teaspoon ground coriander
- 1/2 teaspoon dried chilli flakes
- 1 head of broccoli, cut into small florets
- 4 green onions, thinly sliced
- 80g baby spinach
- 1 cup vegetable or chicken stock
- 1/2 cup coriander sprigs, roughly chopped
- 1/2 cup mint leaves, roughly chopped
- 4 eggs
- 1 cup thick Greek yoghurt
- 1 tablespoon harissa
- Extra mint and coriander leaves, to serve
- Chargrilled sourdough bread, to serve

Method:

1. Heat oil in a large heavy-based frying pan over medium heat. Add leek and capsicum and stir until combined. Cook for 5 minutes or until softened. Stir in cumin, coriander and chilli flakes and cook for 1 minute. Add broccoli, green onion, spinach and stock. Stir until combined. Cover and cook for 2 minutes or until vegetables are just tender. Add chopped coriander and mint. Season with salt and pepper
2. Use a spoon to form indentations in the veggie mixture. Crack an egg into each indent. Cover and cook for 5 minutes or until egg whites are just cooked and the yolk is still wobbly. (It will continue to cook on standing.)
3. Meanwhile, place yoghurt into a bowl. Add harissa, salt and pepper. Swirl harissa through yoghurt. Serve shakshuka immediately, topped with harissa yoghurt and extra herbs with bread on the side

Avocado and Feta Toasts

Prep: 5 Minutes   Serves: 2

Ingredients:

- 1/4 avocado
- 1 teaspoon lemon juice
- 2 thick slices wholegrain toast
- 2 small tomatoes, sliced
- 20g Australian reduced fat feta cheese, crumbled
- 1 tablespoon shredded fresh basil
- Finely grated lemon rind, to taste
- Freshly ground black pepper, to taste

Method:

1. Coarsely mash the avocado and lemon juice together
2. Spread avocado on hot toast, top with tomato and sprinkle with feta and basil. Finely grate a small amount of lemon rind over the toasts and season with pepper

Tips & Hints:
Try omitting the lemon and basil and sprinkling the toast with other flavourings such as: - dukkah - toasted sesame seeds - lemon pepper seasoning - za'atar spice - a sprinkling of cumin.

Avocado and Ricotta Smash on Crusty Sourdough

Prep: 5 Mins   Cook: 20 Mins   Serves: 4

Ingredients:

- 1 ripe avocado, peeled, pitted and cubed
- 250g tub Perfect Italiano Ricotta
- 1/2 lemon
- 3 tbsp extra virgin olive oil
- 4 thick slices sourdough
- 12 cherry tomatoes, on the vine
- 4 soft poached eggs, to serve

Method:

1. Preheat the oven to 200°C. Place the tomatoes onto a tray, season with salt and pepper, and drizzle with 1 tbsp of the olive oil.
2. Place into the oven and roast for 12-15 minutes or until the tomatoes begin to break down and look charred
3. Meanwhile, place the avocado into a medium bowl and coarsely mash. Add the ricotta, a squeeze of lemon juice, and season well with salt and pepper. Gently stir through to mix all ingredients together
4. Toast the sourdough until golden. Spread the ricotta and avocado mix evenly over the slices of hot toast
5. Serve with roasted tomatoes, a poached egg and a drizzle of the remaining olive oil

Tips & Hints:

Add a finely chopped red chili to give a kick to your avocado and ricotta smash.

Eggy French Toast with Berries

Prep: 15 Minutes   Cook: 10 Minutes   Serves: 4

Ingredients:

- 4 large eggs, at room temperature
- 3/4 cup reduced fat milk
- 1/4 cup caster sugar
- 1/2 tsp vanilla extract
- Butter, for greasing pan
- 6-8 slices day-old thick white bread
- Strawberries and blueberries, to serve
- Icing sugar, for dusting

Method:

1. Preheat oven to 120°C/100°C fan-forced. Whisk eggs, milk, sugar and vanilla in a medium shallow dish
2. Grease a large non-stick frying pan with butter and melt over medium heat. Dip 2 bread slices into egg mixture for about 15-20 seconds on each side
3. Add to pan and cook for 2-3 minutes on each side until light golden brown. Transfer to a tray and keep warm in the oven. Repeat with extra butter, remaining bread and egg mixture
4. Place French toast onto serving plates. Top with strawberries and blueberries, lightly dust with icing sugar and serve

Muffin Tin Egg Pies

Prep: 10 Mins   Cook: 20 Mins   Serves: 4

Ingredients:
- 6 large slices sandwich bread, crusts removed
- 40g butter, softened
- 1 tablespoon olive oil
- 1 small brown onion, finely chopped
- 1 small carrot, finely diced
- 125g can corn kernels, drained
- 1/2 cup frozen peas
- 100g double smoked ham or bacon, finely chopped
- 3 eggs
- 1 cup grated tasty cheese

Method:

1. Preheat oven to 180°C. Using a rolling pin, roll slices of bread flat. Spread butter over both sides of bread and press into the moulds of a 1 cup-capacity 6-hole Texas muffin pan. Bake for 15 minutes or until golden and crisp. Set aside to cool
2. Meanwhile, heat the oil in a non-stick frying pan over medium heat. Add onion and carrot and cook for 3 minutes or until softened. Add corn and peas. Remove from heat and stir through ham or bacon. Lightly whisk eggs in a small bowl, then add to vegetable mixture with half the cheese. Season
3. Spoon vegetable mixture into bread shells. Sprinkle with remaining cheese. Bake for 15 minutes or until egg mixture is set and top of pies are golden

Tips & Hints:
These crunchy egg pies are perfect for breakfast on the run or add it to your children's lunchbox for a veggie-filled high-protein bite.

Mini Almond Pancakes

Prep: 10 Minutes   Cook: 10 Minutes   Makes: 12 Pancakes

Ingredients:

- ½ cup (75g) plain flour
- ½ cup (50g) almond meal
- ¾ teaspoon baking powder
- 2 eggs
- 60ml (¼ cup) milk
- 1 teaspoon vanilla extract
- 1 small banana and ¼ cup blueberries mashed together
- 1 ½ tablespoon plain yoghurt
- Ground cinnamon, to sprinkle (optional)

Method:

1. Sift flour and baking powder into a medium bowl. Stir in almond meal. Whisk eggs, milk and vanilla in a jug. Add egg mixture to flour mixture and whisk until well combined
2. Lightly spray a large non-stick frying pan with oil and heat over medium-high heat. Spoon tablespoons of batter into pan to form 4 mini pancakes. Cook for 1-2 minutes each side or until golden and cooked through. Repeat with remaining batter to make 12 pancakes, spraying with a little more oil as required
3. Stir mashed blueberry and banana through yoghurt and serve on top of pancakes
4. Sprinkle over a pinch cinnamon if desired

Tips & Hints:

Leftover pancakes can be wrapped in plastic wrap and frozen for up to 1 month. Try serving topped with apple puree, mashed berries or ricotta.

Gluten Free Apple and Almond Pancakes

Prep: 10 Mins   Cook: 10 Mins   Makes: 8   Serves: 4

Ingredients:

- 2 eggs
- 1/3 cup milk or almond milk
- 1 tablespoon coconut oil, melted
- 1 tablespoon maple syrup, plus extra to serve
- 1 ½ cups almond meal
- 1 teaspoon gluten free baking powder
- ½ cup grated green apple, plus extra sliced to serve
- ½ teaspoon ground cinnamon
- Greek yoghurt and strawberries, to serve
- Natural almonds, roughly chopped, to sprinkle

Method:

1. In a large bowl, whisk eggs, milk, oil and syrup together. Stir in almond meal, baking powder, grated apple and cinnamon. Mix to combine well
2. Heat a large, lightly greased non-stick frying pan over medium heat. Working in batches of 3, pour ¼ cups of batter into the pan. Cook pancakes for 2-3 minutes, until bubbles break on the surface and underside is golden brown. Flip over and cook for 1 minute
3. Serve topped with a dollop of Greek yoghurt, extra sliced apple and berries. Drizzle with extra maple syrup and sprinkle with almonds

Tips & Hints:
- To make this recipe dairy free, use almond milk instead of dairy milk and serve with coconut yoghurt.

Brain-food Cheesy Scrambled Eggs

Prep: 5 Minutes   Cook: 5 Minutes   Serves: 2

Ingredients:

- 4 eggs, at room temperature
- 1/3 cup reduced fat cream
- 1/2 cup shredded tasty cheese
- 1 tablespoon butter
- Wholegrain toast and sliced cherry tomatoes, to serve

Method:

1. Gently whisk eggs, cream and cheese in a bowl. Heat butter in a medium non-stick frying pan over medium heat until foaming
2. Add eggs and swirl over pan base, cook without stirring for 30 seconds, then gently stir egg using a flat-topped spatula for about 2-3 minutes until almost set. Remove from heat
3. Spoon eggs over toast and serve with cherry tomatoes

Mushroom Soufflé Omelette

Prep: 10 Minutes   Cook: 20 Minutes   Serves: 2

Ingredients:

- 1 tablespoon olive oil
- 400g Swiss brown mushrooms, sliced
- Salt and pepper
- 4 eggs
- 2 tablespoons milk
- ¼ teaspoon table salt
- 20g melted butter
- ¼ cup finely grated parmesan
- ¼ cup crème fraiche
- Finely grated parmesan, extra, to serve
- 2 tablespoons finely chopped chives

Method:

1. Heat oil in a large 25cm non-stick frying pan over medium-high heat. Add the mushrooms, season with salt and pepper and cook for 6-7 minutes or until golden. Remove, cover and keep warm. Wipe out the pan.
2. Separate eggs, placing egg yolks into a small bowl and egg whites into a large bowl. Add milk to egg yolks and whisk with a fork. Using a hand beater, whisk egg whites and the ¼ teaspoon salt until stiff peaks form.
3. Heat the frying pan over medium heat. Brush with butter to grease. Using a large metal spoon, gently fold the egg yolks into the egg whites.
4. Pour half the mixture into the pan and cook for 4-5 minutes, or until golden and the eggs are just set. Spoon over half the crème fraiche, parmesan and mushrooms and carefully fold the omelette in half. Cook for 1 minute or until almost set.
5. Transfer to a serving plate (omelette will continue cooking once removed from heat). Repeat using remaining eggs, crème fraiche, cheese and mushrooms. Sprinkle with chives, extra parmesan and pepper to serve.

Baked eggs

Prep: 10 Minutes   Cook: 15 Minutes   Serves: 4

Ingredients:

- 120g baby spinach leaves
- 100g semi-dried tomatoes, chopped
- 70g Danish feta cheese, crumbled
- 2 tablespoons roughly chopped fresh basil
- 4 shallots, thinly sliced
- 1 tablespoon olive oil
- 4 eggs
- Wholegrain toasts (optional), to serve

Method:

1. Preheat the oven to 180°C/160°C. Lightly spray four 1-cup (250ml) capacity ovenproof ramekins with oil
2. Place spinach in a heatproof bowl. Pour ever enough boiling water to cover, set aside for 10 seconds then drain. Once cool enough to handle squeeze out excess water. Combine spinach, tomatoes, feta, basil and shallots in a medium bowl. Divide evenly between prepared dishes, and drizzle each with 1 teaspoon oil. Place dishes on a baking tray and crack an egg on top of each dish
3. Cover with foil and bake for 15 minutes or until egg is cooked to your liking. Season with black pepper. Serve with toast if you like.

Lazy Ladies Loaf

Prep: 10 Min (Plus Chilling & Standing Time)

Ingredients: Cook: 50 Min   Makes: 1 Loaf

- 500gms unbleached plain flour
- 2 teaspoons instant yeast
- 475mls lukewarm water
- 1 teaspoon salt
- Extra flour for dusting and shaping

Method:

1. Mix flour, yeast and salt together in a large bowl
2. Pour in the water to make a sticky dough. Mix together with a spatula until well combined
3. Cover bowl with plastic wrap and leave in the fridge overnight.
4. Next day take out of fridge and rest at room temp for about 1.5 to 2 hours depending on weather (it must be just at room temp before you bake).
5. Line a flat oven tray with baking paper and sprinkle generously with flour. Remove the dough from the bowl using a spatula, scape out onto tray. It will be VERY sticky.
6. Shape dough with floured hands into a ciabatta shape. Flip dough over so that the wrinkled floured side is on top.
7. Place the tray in a cold oven and set at 220 degrees Bake 45 to 50 minutes or until it has a light golden colour and the bread sounds hollow when tapped.
8. Cool on wire racks & serve whilst still warm .

Spinach, Tomato & Egg Pizzas

Prep: 20 Minutes   Cook: 15 Minutes   Serves: 4

Ingredients:

- 1 bunch English spinach, stems trimmed
- 300g fresh ricotta, crumbled
- 4 green onions (shallots), trimmed and thinly sliced
- 2 fresh large pizza bases
- 4 free-range eggs
- 200g heirloom tomatoes or tomato medley, thickly sliced
- ¼ cup small basil leaves
- Extra virgin olive oil, to serve

Method:

1. Preheat oven to 220°C/200°C fan-forced.
2. Wash spinach then plunge into a large saucepan of boiling water, cook for 30 seconds then drain and plunge into iced water to cool. Drain again and squeeze out excess moisture. Roughly chop spinach.
3. Combine spinach, ricotta and green onions in a medium bowl.
4. Place pizza bases onto lightly greased baking trays. Evenly top each with spinach mixture.
5. Crack 2 eggs on top of each pizza. Bake for 12-15 minutes or until crust is crisp and eggs are just set.
6. Scatter with tomatoes and basil leaves. Drizzle with extra virgin olive oil. Season with salt and pepper and serve.

Avo Bowla-Rama

Prep: 10 Minutes　　　　　　　　Serves: 2

Ingredients:

- 50g frozen acai pulp (see note)
- 1 frozen banana
- 1/2 cup frozen blueberries
- 50ml apple juice
- 1 avocado, sliced
- 1/4 cup fresh blueberries
- 1/2 mango, sliced
- 2 tbs granola
- 1 tsp hemp seeds

Method:

1. Place acai pulp, frozen banana, frozen blueberries, apple juice and half the avocado in the bowl of a food processor and process until smooth
2. Top with remaining avocado, fresh blueberries and mango. Sprinkle with granola and hemp seeds to serve

Tips & Hints:

Frozen acai pulp is made from small, purple berries that grow on palm trees native to South America. It is available in the freezer section of major supermarkets

Cloud Eggs with Pancetta Crumbs and Gruyere

Prep: 15 Mins   Cook: 20 Mins   Serves: 4

Ingredients:

- 4 thin slices pancetta
- 4 eggs
- 1/2 tsp salt
- 50g gruyere cheese, finely grated
- Chervil sprigs, to serve

Method:

1. Preheat oven to 180°C. Line a baking tray with baking paper. Bake pancetta for 10-15 minutes or until golden. Cool on tray. Finely chop pancetta and set aside
2. Separate eggs and place egg whites into a bowl. Add salt and beat until stiff peaks form. Add cornflour and beat until combined.
3. Spoon egg white onto prepared tray forming nest shapes. Form an indentation in the centre. Place egg yolks into centre of nests. Lightly cover nests with baking paper and foil.
4. Bake for 15-20 minutes or until nests are just set. Serve eggs sprinkled with pancetta crumbs, gruyere cheese and chervil sprigs

Savoury Breakfast Tarts

Prep: 15 Mins Cook: 30 Mins Makes: 6

Ingredients:

- 3 sheets frozen ready rolled puff pastry, partially thawed
- 1 tbs olive oil
- 150g cup mushrooms, finely chopped
- 8 sprigs lemon thyme, leaves removed
- Sea salt flakes and freshly ground black pepper
- 1/3 cup fresh ricotta
- 12 small eggs
- Olive oil cooking spray
- 250g small vine ripened tomatoes
- Extra sprigs lemon thyme, to serve

Method:

1. Preheat oven to 200°C. Grease 12 patty pan moulds. Cut 12 x 9.5cm rounds from pastry using a scone cutter and place into prepared patty pan tray. Prick base of pastry with a fork. Place in freezer for 10 minutes. Bake for 10-15 minutes or until lightly browned. Cool. Reduce oven temperature to 180°C
2. Heat oil in a frying pan over a high heat. Add mushrooms and lemon thyme leaves. Season with salt and pepper. Cook, stirring often, for 10 minutes or until golden. Transfer to a bowl and cool
3. Add ricotta to mushrooms mixture and stir until well combined. Spoon 3 tsp of mushroom mixture into tarts, spreading up sides to form a dent in the centre. Separate eggs. Place yolks into the centre of tarts. (Egg whites can be place in an airtight container and frozen for later use). Spray tarts with olive oil and loosely cover with foil. Bake for 15-20 minutes or until egg is just set
4. Meanwhile, line a baking tray with baking paper. Place tomatoes onto prepared tray and spray with olive oil and season with salt. Roast for 15 minutes or until softened. Serve tarts garnished with extra lemon thyme and roasted tomatoes

Smokey Butter Beans with Tomato and Chorizo

Prep: 15 Mins   Cook: 20 Mins   Serves: 4

Ingredients:

- 2 tsp olive oil
- 1 small onion, finely chopped
- 2 chorizo sausages, chopped
- 1 garlic clove, crushed
- 2 tsp smoked paprika
- 400g can Ardmona Rich & Thick Classic Tomatoes
- 2 x 400g cans butter beans, drained, rinsed
- 1/2 cup chicken stock
- Chopped chives or parsley and buttered toast, to serve

Method:

1. Heat oil in a large non-stick frying pan over medium heat. Add onion, chorizo and garlic. Cook, stirring often, for 4-5 minutes until onion is very tender. Stir in paprika. Cook for 30 seconds
2. Add tomatoes, beans and stock. Simmer, uncovered, over medium-low heat for 10-12 minutes until thick. Sprinkle with chives or parsley. Serve with buttered toast

Frittata Caprese with spinach, tomato and ricotta

Prep: 5 Minutes Cook: 30 Minutes Serves: 4

Ingredients:

- 1 tablespoon olive oil
- 250g mini roma tomatoes, halved
- 6 sprigs oregano
- Salt and pepper, to season
- 4 cups baby spinach leaves
- 8 eggs
- ½ cup single cream
- ½ cup finely grated parmesan, plus extra to serve
- 1 cup (240g) ricotta
- Basil leaves, to serve

Method:

1. Preheat oven to 220°C (200°C fan forced). Heat oil in a 25cm non-stick oven proof frying pan over medium heat. Add tomato, oregano, salt and pepper and cook, stirring, for 1 minute. Add the spinach and cook for 30 seconds, or until wilted.
2. Whisk together the eggs, cream, parmesan, salt and pepper and pour into the pan. Move the mix around gently with a spatula to cover the base underneath the tomato mixture.
3. Spoon over the ricotta. Transfer to oven and cook for 20-25 minutes or until golden and set. Set aside for 5 minutes to cool slightly. Scatter with basil leaves and the extra parmesan.

Mexican Pan Frittata

Prep: 20 Minutes Cook: 25 Minutes Serves: 4

Ingredients:

- 2 tbs olive oil
- 1 small red onion, halved, thinly sliced
- 2 garlic cloves, finely chopped
- 1 yellow or red capsicum, halved, deseeded, sliced
- 1 cob sweet corn, kernels removed
- 1/3 cup coriander leaves, chopped
- 200g mini roma tomatoes, halved lengthways
- 8 large eggs, at room temperature
- Store-bought tomato salsa, diced avocado, coriander leaves & lime wedges, to serve

Method:

1. Preheat grill on medium-high. Heat oil over medium heat in a 20cm non-stick ovenproof frying pan with oil. Add onion and garlic and cook for 3-4 minutes until soft. Add capsicum and corn, cook, stirring often, for 4-5 minutes until capsicum softens. Stir in chopped coriander
2. Spread mixture evenly over the base of pan. Scatter tomatoes over mixture. Whisk eggs in a jug. Pour egg mixture over vegetables. Shake the pan to evenly distribute egg. Reduce heat to medium-low and cook for 8-10 minutes or until almost set
3. Place pan under hot grill for 3-5 minutes or until top just sets. Stand for 5 minutes then transfer to a board. Cut into wedges. Serve with tomato salsa, avocado, coriander and lime wedges

www.ingramcontent.com/pod-product-compliance
Lightning Source LLC
Chambersburg PA
CBHW081627100526
44590CB00021B/3632